# IT'S TIME TO EAT A CHERRY TOMATO

# It's Time to Eat a Cherry Tomato

## Walter the Educator

**SKB**

Silent King Books
A WhichHead Entertainment Imprint

Disclaimer

It's Time to Eat a Cherry Tomato is a
collectible early learning book by Walter
the Educator suitable for all ages
belonging to Walter the Educator's Time
to Eat Book Series. Collect more books at
WaltertheEducator.com


**USE THE EXTRA SPACE TO TAKE NOTES
AND DOCUMENT YOUR MEMORIES**

# CHERRY TOMATO

It's time to eat, what a treat,

# It's Time to Eat a

# Cherry

# Tomato

A little red ball that's fun to meet!

Shiny and round, it's ready to go,

A cherry tomato, let's start the show!

Picked from the garden, fresh and bright,

It sparkles in the morning light.

I hold it gently in my hand,

Like a treasure from the summer land.

Oh, cherry tomato, juicy and sweet,

You're such a tasty snack to eat!

Pop you in, and what a surprise

A burst of flavor, right before my eyes!

Like a tiny sun, glowing with pride,

You're red on the outside, all soft inside.

I take a bite—what do I see?

Seeds like little stars, dancing free!

It's Time to Eat a

# Cherry Tomato

You taste of sunshine, warm and mild,

Making me feel so happy and wild.

With every crunch, with every chew,

It's like a party, just for you!

Oh, cherry tomato, juicy and sweet,

You're such a tasty snack to eat!

Pop you in, and what a surprise

A burst of flavor, right before my eyes!

Sometimes you're on a salad plate,

Sometimes you're lunch, and you taste great!

On sandwiches or all alone,

You're the best snack I've ever known.

You're not too big, not too small,

Just the right size for me to hold and call.

I can eat you with one big bite,

Or nibble slowly, both feel right!

I love your color, your shiny skin,

When I pop you in my mouth, I grin!

One after one, you're such a treat,

## It's Time to Eat a

# Cherry

# Tomato

A cherry tomato, crisp and sweet.

Oh, cherry tomato, juicy and sweet,

You're such a tasty snack to eat!

Pop you in, and what a surprise—

A burst of flavor, right before my eyes!

# ABOUT THE CREATOR

Walter the Educator is one of the pseudonyms for Walter Anderson. Formally educated in Chemistry, Business, and Education, he is an educator, an author, a diverse entrepreneur, and he is the son of a disabled war veteran. "Walter the Educator" shares his time between educating and creating. He holds interests and owns several creative projects that entertain, enlighten, enhance, and educate, hoping to inspire and motivate you. Follow, find new works, and stay up to date with Walter the Educator™

at WaltertheEducator.com

Milton Keynes UK
Ingram Content Group UK Ltd.
UKHW021937281024
450365UK00018B/1144

9 798330 495382